YOUR KNOWLEDGE HAS VALUE

- We will publish your bachelor's and
  master's thesis, essays and papers

- Your own eBook and book -
  sold worldwide in all relevant shops

- Earn money with each sale

Upload your text at www.GRIN.com
and publish for free

Bibliographic information published by the German National Library:

The German National Library lists this publication in the National Bibliography;
detailed bibliographic data are available on the Internet at http://dnb.dnb.de .

Imprint:

Copyright © 2010 GRIN Verlag, Open Publishing GmbH
Print and binding: Books on Demand GmbH, Norderstedt Germany
ISBN: 978-3-668-11074-8

George Harding III

Customer Service Importance. Various Perspectives on Where Society Stands

GRIN Publishing

Review of Literature

Historical Background and Related State-of-the-Art Concepts

Anyone can provide customer service. It's simple. Basically, one just have to 'hear' what the customer wants and be aware of their needs, and then explores many different alternatives, to come up with possible solutions to fulfill that want or need. Even better, it takes someone really special to actually 'listen' to provide an exceptional customer service experience; one that is of supererogatory substance, and one that goes beyond the normal call of duty. This concept can apply to all types of organizations from the sole proprietors to the business partners to the different governments and their agencies to the large corporations. No professional or business is exempt from provide quality service to their consumers or constituents. Customer service can be provided from many different media outlets. Customer service can be given from one's very doorstep with their daily newspaper to overseas in a call center in Bangkok. One thing for sure that does hold truth is that once a customer feels valued for the money they are spending on a product or service, they will be more likely to return to that same provider and/or organization. To commence, this Literature Review pertains to the different outlooks of what customer service, the standards of customer service per industry, and the rewards of providing excellent customer service for the individual, the organization's culture, and the customer being impacted as well. In order to better understand how important a customer service experience can affect both the company's image and their customer perspective in both a negative or positive way, we must first understand what customer service is defined as.

There are several of different perceptions of what customer service should and should not be. To the student intern, customer service involves making a commitment to learning what the customer's needs and wants are and finding a plan of action that will put into practice customer friendly processes and solutions beyond the customer's expectation level. The student is a firm believer that the consumer should not be merely treated as a means to end, but as valued customer. Without any customer, an organization would not be in business. Now the student wouldn't go as far to say that the customer is always right, but even when the customer may be wrong, their needs should be met and their understanding of the situation should be clarified. A business should always build rapport with their customer. They must establish a relationship of integrity and trust with their local community and expand from there. In "8 Rules for Good Customer Service," Susan Ward (2010) explains how to go about forming such a relationship. She says that one can successfully accomplish this "by remembering one true secret of good customer service and acting accordingly; 'You will be judged by what you do, not what you say.'" This is so true. Actions do speak louder the words. This applies universally throughout many general concepts as well. Sure it is wonderful to hear all the nice rewards that a business can offer someone, but it is the actually happening that will retain the customer base.

If a business truly wants to retain their customer base, they must "make their customers feel important and appreciated" (Friedman, 2010). Also in her article, Susan Friedman, writer of "The Ten Commandments of Great Customer Service, writes that being a good listener, identifying and anticipating needs, and helping the customer understand the business' systems are great ways of providing excellent service. Some other commandments that the student intern concurs on in this article are 'knowing how to apologize,' 'giving more than expected,' and 'treating the employees well' (Friedman, 2010). If an applicant is someone that rarely takes responsibility for their own actions and refuses to apologize for the inflections on others then they would not make a pretty good customer service representative. Moreover, treating the employees well will more than likely transfer into the kind of service that the representative will provide to the customer base. Some of the functions that representatives perform are utilizing information to solve problems, make changes to accounts within their power, and abide by specified guidelines for requests and customer complaints. If an issue goes beyond the representative control then a representative of higher position such as supervisor or team lead may have to be consulted and inevitably, provide assistance. To ensure quality of service is being recorded, representatives are constantly be monitored, listened to by their supervisor, QA (quality assurance), and/or call center manager. Outside of call center, representatives are being watched and carefully evaluated by their higher-ups in order to ensure quality service face-to-face with a customer. Most representatives use computers, headphones, phones, and many types of software in their daily work.

Knowing the functions that they can and cannot perform can make a customer run as smoothly as possible. If a representative actively listens to a customer's concern and knows that what this customer needs is beyond his control, he/ she will instantly know what or where to direct the customer in order to successful work toward getting that concern addressed. After actively listening to customer and the representative discovers that the concern can be resolved within their own hands, this gives the rep encouragement to do what they need to do in order to fulfill this concern. "Customer-service reps are most effective when they feel empowered to solve customer problems as they see fit, and not reprimanded for having complaints in the first place. They should be rewarded for solving problems and pleasing customers and there should be demerits when they don't" (Spors, 2008). If a representative isn't actively listening to the customer, then this is when the demerits should be warranted. Active listening is part of a representative position. This should never be compromised. Customers that are not being actively listened to are being neglected and not paid enough attention towards. This is unacceptable on any level, professionally or otherwise. This type of behavior would eventually lead to outsourcing of jobs to other countries to save money on the business part. "Outsourcing saves the company money, but it forces the customers to deal with people who may not speak English well" (Hammitt, 2006). This can be very frustrating for the customer and even more damaging, this may push away many customers to other competitors. Customer service should not be taken lightly. It has become more and more increasingly important to feel appreciated for one's choice of where he/she give their money. It is not all about sales anymore, it's the connotation that one feels when they hear or see a particular brand name when mentioned.

Each firm has their own particular customer service standards. Firms that operate effective organizations are good for developing a set of written customer service standards. Their standards serve as objectives and provide a chart in comparison on which results can be measured for future references. These standards are partly based on the customer's needs; at least they are supposed to be. It is very necessary to know what one's competitor is offering in relation to products, services, and incentives for both the customer and their employees. Remember, the employee are often time the frontline person or gatekeeper, the representative of the organization, and the mirror reflection of their image to the consumers. In 2000, the Revco Drug Store started a customer service program to define some improvements based on a slogan, "Every customer, every time" (Morrow, 2000). With this slogan, they implemented a three behavior process that every employee could act upon. The first behavior in this article is greeting customers every time they enter the store. So this means that if the same customer comes in the store 5 times that day, they should be spoken to by at least one of employees within the organization each and every time they came inside store. The second behavior is every time a salesperson sees a customer searching for a product; the employee is to ask the customer if they need assistance. This would show the customer that they are being paid attention to and may even give them the realization that they are in a place where the people care enough to ask. One never knows where just merely asking will get them. The last behavior in this article is to make eye contact with customers every time you speak to them. Customers are willing to pay more for better service. This company evaluates their progress with that new set of improvements by the use of mystery shoppers. Once these standards are set, there will be an on-going system of evaluation that should follow. Revco Drug Stores turned their slogan into "a way of doing business because the service standards were specially stated and then measured on a regular basis" (Morrow, 2000).

Customer service standards will differ by type of industry as well. Some examples of the current trends of customer service standards per an industry appears in wholesaling in which at least 98 percent of orders are filled accurately or that in manufacturing the order cycle time is no more than five days. In the retailer industry, it is customary to be able to make a return within 30 days. Another is with airliners in which they are expected to at least have 90 percent of arrivals on time. Truckers should only have a maximum of 5 percent loss and damage per year. Even the restaurant industry is supposed to serve lunch within five minutes of the order being placed. A very small percentage of increase attention to customer service satisfaction can yield a large amount of money of additional revenue to a company. In the "Top Ten Customer Service Standards" by Brad Hulsken (2007), he stated that "the goal, every time we serve a customer, is to develop a friend not just a customer for today." They are working to develop a friend and the customer for life. This is a perfect example of how an organization is utilizing attention to customer and actively listening. The student intern can align along comfortably with the standards listed in this article that outlines that "if you say it, do it," "keep your personal problems out of the business," "offer your name, get their name, and use it," "dressing professionally,", "give them you full, complete, undivided attention," "be enthusiastic", "smiles and smiles a lot- show teeth," "making the buying experience fun- for the customer and you," "treat people as you would want to be treated", and "Go the extra mile! Do something different or extraordinary to set yourself apart" (Hulsken, 2007). Having standards in customer service couldn't be said any better. These standards above are an example of not only someone that provides customer service, but exceptional customer service. The customer will have no reason to waiver or discontinue a relationship with the organization.

Besides the for-profit organizations having service standards, there are governmental agencies that utilize customer service standards similarly. The U.S. Census Bureau has a code of customer service standards in which they break down their groups of customers into 4 categories. These categories are the "general information customers, purchasers of the off-the-shelf products, special request customers, and the survey sponsors" (U.S. Census, 1999).

The standards of the Census Bureau are of excellence, timeliness, responsiveness, accessibility, and commitment. They do guarantee a quality product or service that meets or exceeds one's expectations, to provide one with realistic delivery times based on the nature of the request, and they will respond promptly to all requests in accord with their resources and capabilities. Lastly, they will provide one with choices for products, services, and the means of delivery and will be courteous, respectful, responsible, and professional as outlined on their website. The Census Bureau is very serious about these standards; so serious that they are in accordance with the Government Performance and Results Act of 1993 by measuring up its standards and publishing them as well annually. These are just a few customer service standards that organizations abide or should abide by in order to stay legal and in the marketplace as a fair competitor.

As a fellow CSR, the student intern knows that one may have to deal with difficult customers daily. This can be very challenging. With that said, the "ability to resolve customer's problem has the potential to be very rewarding" as well (Bureau of Labor Statistics, 2010). The student intern deals with multiple types of customers every single day and finds that the most part of perform his duties is the gratitude that the customers shows afterwards. This is a feeling of accomplishment is very rewarding. This feeling motivates the representatives to continue with a brilliant job and brings them back the next day. Though this is usually the frontline reward received from serving the customers, there are concrete rewards also. "Spending on customer satisfaction measurement services during 2003 was expected to exceed $600 million" according to Inside Research, a marketing research industry newsletter (Kiska, 2004). From the intern's experience at previous customer positions, companies will budget for the research that will tell them how to motivate their employees who will in turn provide exceptional customer service to the customer which would ensure customer satisfaction and a continued relationship with that business. The student intern has taken customer service simulations, personality tests, and participated in all types of performance pay programs mandated by his previous employers. The following factors are outlined in the HR Magazine in February 2004 by John Kista:

* Understand what its customers expect.

* Understand how customer satisfaction affects organizational success.

* Develop and implement a valid customer survey.

* Assure employees that the metrics used are valid.

* Consider whether additional factors should affect rewards.

* Balance customer satisfaction with employee productivity and return on investment.

These requirements are necessary in order to have a successful, effective performance pay program. Some reasons why companies do choose to reward their employees, from top to the bottom, can vary, but one thing is certain; they are all based on customer satisfaction. Vafa Akhavan, executive director of consulting at J.D. Power & Associates, stated that linking performance pay to customer satisfaction will "develop employee behaviors that are required to build and nurture an organizational culture centered on customer service" (Kiska, 2004). Bottom line is that if a business keeps their employees happy than shall be their customer bases overall.

Some examples of companies with culture geared at this notion of utilizing performance pay programs to ensure customer satisfactions are Zappos.com and Frosch Rewards. At Zappos, the CEO believes that "if you get the right culture, most of the other stuff- the great customer service, or the building a great long-term brand, or passionate employees and customers- will happen naturally on its own" (Zappos, 2009). If one's household is in practical order, then beautiful things will blossom from one's doorstep. When reporters comes out and visit the Zappos office, they are free to speak with anyone, not just selected individuals like most companies. This shows that this company is open and honest while their employees are well-pleased. This can prove to be very rewarding for the fellow employees. Some of Zappos' core values are delivering WOW through service, embracing and driving change, the creation of fun and a little weirdness, being adventurous, creative, and open-minded, building open and honest communications, be passionate and determined, and being humble. Why in the world wouldn't someone want to work for a company of such culture? Frosch Rewards is a business in which specialize in creating employee rewards and incentives for a multitude of different organizations. Frosch views "reward and "recognition" independently not as one in the same. To Frosch, an employee reward program involves "the system 'set-up' by an organization to motivate, inspire, and rewards its employees," and recognition is "not just something nice to do" in their company. (Frosch, 2007). The employee recognition program includes "a system 'set-up' by an organization to recognize the desired behavior conducive to the company's business objectives and to encourage more of the desired behavior" (Frosch, 2007).This same concept is applied to everyone as a child through grade school. One would be recognized for perfect attendance or an all 'A' honor roll. All this does is let the employees know that the company is paying attention to them and their actions that are aligned well with the company's culture. When others are recognize for their behavior, this makes others want to be recognize as well so they will do whatever it may take to accomplish that recognition, or often time, monetary rewards.

Ron Zemke of Service America once stated that "reward, whether in the coin of the realm or the psyche of the recipient, is critical to a service improvement program" (Hess, 2009). It is of the upmost importance that there is a reward at the beginning, during, and at the end of honest, hard-working day of an employee in order to see the end of results as customer satisfaction. In the article, "Service Incentives," the actual amount of the reward isn't important, but "the key is to catch employees in the act of doing things right and awarding them accordingly" (Hess, 2009). If a company does constantly focused on the amount of the rewards only, instead of why this reward is given to begin with, then their reward program will not be as effective as expected. Some higher ups feels that employees shouldn't be rewarded for the job that they are expected to do, but often sometimes, those employees need those rewards or recognition in order to build and retain confidence that would translate into better customer service experiences for all. Cumulative and time off bonuses, a call of thanks from the CEO, cash-on-the-spot monetary rewards, dinner or theater tickets, or a special meal in the executive dining room are examples of some ways of rewarding those employees that behavior exhibits those of the company's culture. Though rewards only can only attempt to seek to retain a good group of team players that are customer service-oriented by nature and culture alike, employees must be recognize for their power within the organization. This concept is realized in the article titled, "Thinking Managers: Rewards and incentives- when self-interest isn't enough." The main lesson revealed from the article is that rewards alone aren't enough to retain employees and their loyalty. Without a solid, on-going set of loyal employees, the goal of customer satisfaction and an overall boast to the ROI are threatened. How customer satisfaction would be threatened is by the budget. Much more finances would be directed toward training of new employees than the research into employee incentives. Moreover, if the employees aren't happy, there may be a very good chance that the customer bases may not be as well. The student intern will conclude with this quote that shall sum up this third section of this Literature Review. "The bonus kings of banks and big business will perhaps in time come to understand their dependence on the people in every organization who possess other talents and without whose contribution nothing great can be achieved – and whose true value cannot be measured in money alone" (Heller, 2009).

Need for Internship Activity

Do we truly want a future where the money we spend isn't valued? We are amidst a historical turning point where every generation will be affected in a positive or negative fashion which is up to us. There is a great immediate need for the project. As our economy play roller coaster with our finances, it has become even more increasing important that we as a society watch were we are spending our income. Business that do offer appreciation and gratitude that we as consumers are doing business with them, deserve our attention. Those that only focused on just making money and not worried about the customer satisfaction they should be providing needs to be put on the backburner until they learn to value the business that consumers bring to them in order to keep their doors open. People need to open their eyes to the rising cost and the decrease of service. If we don't do anything now, find a way to thoroughly communicate and evaluate our spending in relation to value of customer service, and then we will be in store for a future of high rates and no service. With the successful completion of this proposed activity, Emmis Austin will have a greater number of listenership and take a look within their own organization to see what they can do better to serve our community. Maybe they will even consider a customer week where they can explore what their local community's wants and needs while also giving voluntarily to improving their public image if applicable.

References

Bureau of Labor Statistics. *Customer Service Representatives.* Retrieved Feb 1, 2010 from

http://www.bls.gov/oco/ocos280.htm

Customer Service Week. *Welcome to CSWeek.com.* (n.d.). Retrieved Jan 28, 2010 from

http://www.csweek.com/customer_service_week.php

Friedman, Susan. *The Ten Commandments of Great Customer Service.* (n.d). Retrieved Feb 1, 2010 from http://marketing.about.com/od/relationshipmarketing/a/crmtopten.htm

Frosch Rewards and Incentives. *Employee Reward & Recognition Programs.* (n.d.). Retrieved Feb 3, 2010 from http://www.froschincentives.com/solutions-employee.do

H, Tony. *Your Culture Is Your Brand.* Jan 2009.

http://blogs.zappos.com/blogs/ceo-and-coo-blog/2009/01/03/your-culture-is-your-brand

Hammit, J. *Customer Service Problems and Trends.* June 2006. http://www.associatedcontent.com/article/36075/customer_service_problems_and_trends.html?cat=3

Heller, Robert. *Rewards and incentives - when self-interest isn't enough.* Mar 2009. http://www.management-issues.com/2009/3/20/opinion/rewards-and-incentives----when-self-interest-isnt-enough.asp

Hess, J. *Service Incentives.* (n.d.). Retrieved Feb 1, 2010 from http://www.customerperspectives.com/articles/customer-service-incentives.htm

Hulsken, Brad. *Top Ten Customer Service Standards.* Retrieved Feb 1, 2010 from http://www.expertbusinesssource.com/blog/1270000327/post/1450014745.html

Kiska, J. *Customer satisfaction pays off rewards can motivate employees to deliver top-notch customer service.* Feb 2004. http://findarticles.com/p/articles/mi_m3495/is_2_49/ai_n6040868/

Morrow, Peggy. *Setting and Measuring Service Standards.* Aug 2000. http://www.inc.com/articles/2000/08/20029.html

Office of Management and Budget. *Government Performance and Results Act of 1993.*

http://www.whitehouse.gov/omb/mgmt-gpra_gplaw2m/

Spors, K. *Getting at the Root of Your Customer-Service Problems*. Sept 2008.

http://blogs.wsj.com/independentstreet/2008/09/22/getting-at-the-root-of-your-customer-service-problems/tab/article/

Ward, Susan. *8 Rules For Good Customer Service*. (n.d) Retrieved Feb 1, 2010 from
http://sbinfocanada.about.com/od/relationshipmarketing/a/custservrules.htm

U.S. Census Bureau. *Customer Service Standards*. Aug 2008.
http://www.census.gov/mso/www/custstd.html

YOUR KNOWLEDGE HAS VALUE

- We will publish your bachelor's and
  master's thesis, essays and papers

- Your own eBook and book -
  sold worldwide in all relevant shops

- Earn money with each sale

Upload your text at www.GRIN.com
and publish for free